RAILWAYS AROUND BRIGHTON

IN THE 1970s AND 1980s

Andy Gibbs

AMBERLEY

First published 2020

Amberley Publishing
The Hill, Stroud
Gloucestershire, GL5 4EP

www.amberley-books.com

Copyright © Andy Gibbs, 2020

The right of Andy Gibbs to be identified as
the Author of this work has been asserted in
accordance with the Copyrights, Designs and
Patents Act 1988.

ISBN 978 1 4456 8191 7 (print)
ISBN 978 1 4456 8192 4 (ebook)

British Library Cataloguing in Publication Data.
A catalogue record for this book is available from
the British Library.

Typesetting by SJmagic DESIGN SERVICES, India.
Printed in the UK.

Introduction

Welcome to this, my sixth book. *Railways Around Brighton* puts me firmly back in my former home territory. I touched briefly on the Brighton area in *The Southern Region in the 1970s and 1980s*, but this will cover the area in greater depth.

While the area is synonymous with EMUs and commuter trains, the limited freight and parcels traffic did make a welcome relief. There was also a large number of excursion trains to the South Coast resorts and later the reintroduction of direct services to the Midlands and North West brought yet more variety. Saturdays also saw the running of loco-hauled trains to Exeter and Bristol. All of this is included.

We will start off at Brighton before heading up the mainline to Gatwick, then return to Brighton and head east towards Seaford and Hastings and DEMU territory. Finally, we run down the Mid Sussex line to the coast and return towards Brighton.

This is my record of the changing railway scene, with many images taken by me around the city and throughout Sussex.

Working for British Rail gave me access to some never repeated photo opportunities, or even just a tip off that something special was running.

As the Brighton mainline runs more or less directly north–south, finding good photo locations was often an issue as you would be shooting into the sun. You'll find several photos taken from Dyke Rd Drive bridge, in Brighton, and also from Mill Road in Patcham. Mill Road was probably my favourite location in the city for photos especially on a warm summer's day ... just keep a look out for the adders!

At many of the photo locations it is now impossible to take photographs due to development, high palisade fencing or the encroachment of vegetation.

This album will take you back to a time when the trains were blue, like the saucy postcards from the seafront shops. Most images are from the heyday of BR Blue the 1970s and 1980s, plus a few from a little earlier.

Most images are scanned from 35 mm transparencies with some 35 mm black and white images and medium-format black and white negatives and slides.

Many of the images are taken by me, but thanks are due to the photographers who captured some never to be repeated images. I always enjoy the research for these books and a number of websites always come up trumps for information. These include, in no particular order, Six Bells Junction, Rail Gen Archive, SEMG online, Blood and Custard, and The Bashing Years. Many thanks to you all.

The beer of choice to celebrate finishing this book has been a nice bottle of Harvey's Sussex Best.

I hope you enjoy the journey around Sussex.

Andy Gibbs,
March 2020

We start off with the other railway in Brighton; Volks Electric Railway on the seafront. Opened in 1883 the railway has been running for nearly 140 years. Back in 1983 my late father, Fred, was a driver on the railway for a couple of years, after he had retired from Southdown. Wrapped up as if it was mid-winter, we find him and car 3 heading towards Black Rock. The photo was taken by my late Uncle Tony whose many railway images adorn my books. Taken on 12 April 1982. (J. A. Lower)

In wet conditions 4VEP 7804 waits to depart with a stopping service to Portsmouth Harbour. In the background can be seen unidentified 4CAP, 4BEP and 4CIG units. Taken on 6 May 1982.

Brighton and 2HAP 6042 is captured at a deserted, apart from staff, platform 1. A sister 2HAP units sits in platform two. Taken on 6 May 1982.

No. 50001 *Dreadnought* grumbles away at Brighton with 1V61, the 09.20 Saturdays only service to Exeter St Davids. This was the first time that a Class 50 had worked the service which had been the mainstay of Class 33s for many years. The service was also diverted via Chandlers Ford this day due to engineering work. Taken on 11 October 1980. (A. Gibbs)

A frosty March morning sees No. 33012 at the head of 1V22, the 08.20 Saturdays only Brighton to Cardiff service. No. 47437 has charge of 1M50, the 08.47 to Manchester Piccadilly. Taken on March 1984. (A. Gibbs)

A very quiet Brighton station sees 2HAP unit 6053 and two sister units on platform 2 waiting for their next service. Taken on 7 October 1981.

An unusual visitor to Brighton; not the Class 33 but the 4TC sets behind it. No. 33110 and 4TC sets 8027 and 8017 are working a football charter to Pokesdown. Brighton are away to Bournemouth. The result; Bournemouth 0 Brighton 2. Up the Albion! Taken on 2 December 1989.

A gloomy Brighton station and preserved 4SUB unit 4732 is working the LCGB 'Seaside Sub' railtour. In the adjacent platform is 4CAP unit 3307, formally 2HAP units 6060 and 6073. Taken on 26 February 1983.

No. 33027 *Earl Mountbatten of Burma* propels the stock for 1V46, the 08.30 to Cardiff Central off the West Car Road and into Brighton station. An unidentified named Class 47 is berthed in Montpelier sidings. Taken on 13 May 1988.

Taken from Howard Place this gives an overall view of the station and the hilly nature of Brighton. Class 33 No. 6565 (later 33047) and Class 08 No. 3220 (later 08173) can be seen along with unidentified Class 73, 4CIG, 4VEP and 5BEL units. The car park is very empty so it was probably a weekend. Taken in 1972. (J. A. M. Vaughan)

The loco sidings at Brighton and three unidentified Class 73s wait for their next duty. The one closest to the camera has worked the Eastbourne newspaper and van train, headcode 43. An old Hillman Minx can also be glimpsed to the left. Taken on 6 May 1982.

In the middle road at Brighton, No. 73005 looks like its been in the wars with the dents and scrape marks around the cab. Taken in 1980. (R. Marsh)

Stormy skies at Brighton as No. 33211 and unidentified Class 33 and 73s are berthed in the loco sidings. The signal box looms over the stock in Montpelier sidings. Taken on 26 September 1982. (R. Marsh)

Platform 1 at Brighton and we find No. 47145 having arrived with an unidentified Merrymaker train. These were excursion trains run by British Rail and were fantastic value for money. Taken in 1979. (R. Marsh)

No. 73116 *Selhurst* in ex-works condition with an unidentified service, formed of Mk I stock. Taken in December 1986.

Brighton station roof has had several major refurbishments over the years. With the western trainshed covered in scaffolding, 2HAP No. 6081 departs en route to Littlehampton. Taken on 6 May 1982.

No. 33055 departs from Brighton light engine. Taken in May 1979. (J. A. Lower)

The motor coaches of 5BEL unit 3053 were stored at Brighton for many years. Here they are seen in Montpelier sidings sandwiching S12529S, the buffet car, from 4BUF unit 3084. This vehicle was claimed for the National Collection but was damaged by fire at the Nene Valley Railway in 1978 and eventually cut up. Taken on 7 September 1977.

In the wall sidings at Brighton we find electro-diesel No. 73140 berthed between duties. Taken on 21 August 1985.

In ex-works condition is 4BEP unit 7017 seen here in Montpelier sidings. Taken on May 1979. (J. A. Lower)

The platform indicator board at Brighton before electronics! All hand operated and now at the late Sir Robert McAlpine's Fawley Hill. It can often be seen in the background during episodes of the *Great Model Railway Challenge* TV show. The blackboard shows that the Newhaven to Dieppe Sealink ferry service is suspended until further notice. This is probably due to strike action caused by a threat to withdraw the ferry Senlac from the route. Taken on 30 January 1982.

The MLVs were not common visitors to Brighton until a new contract to move American Express documents was started in the mid-1980s. Unit 9009 in 'Jaffa Cake' livery is berthed in Montpelier sidings along with preserved 2BIL unit 2090. Taken in January 1989. (K. R. Carter)

No. 33038 and 3R DEMUs 1203 and 1206 make for an interesting combination as they form the Southern Electric Groups 'Inter Village Express' railtour. Taken on 6 May 1979.

With the secondman hanging out of the window No. 73120 runs light engine past Brighton signal box and into the station. The marks in the end wall are where Brighton locomotive works abutted the building. Taken in August 1981. (M. Howarth)

The Central division had a small allocation of 4CEP and 4BEP units. We find unit 7101 on the London end of a train at Brighton.

Brighton's local newspaper *The Evening Argus* has always had a love/hate relationship with the railway, which continues even today. However, to celebrate the papers centenary British Rail named No. 73101 *Brighton Evening Argus* and renumbered it to 73100 for a while. Here the loco is seen shortly after the naming ceremony. Taken on 3 December 1980. (A. Gibbs)

May 1979 saw a pair of cross-country trains introduced between Manchester and Brighton. In 1982 we find No. 47054 waiting depart with 1M64, the 15.00 departure to Manchester Piccadilly. Taken on 6 August 1982.

No. 73122 *County of East Sussex* approaches Brighton station with the Royal train conveying the Queen. Shame the policeman got in the way of this photo, but he does nicely frame the loco and the two Rover SD1s. Taken on 16 July 1985. (A. Gibbs)

It's a wet summer's day as ScotRail-liveried No. 47462 *Charles Rennie Mackintosh* waits to depart from Brighton with 1S87, the 13.15 to Glasgow and Edinburgh, 'The Sussex Scot'. This was the first year this service had operated, the following year it was moved to a morning departure. Taken on 26 August 1988.

No. 47183 idles away in Brighton station with a rake of largely Mk II stock forming an unidentified return excursion train. Taken on May 1976. (A. Edwards)

For a few days in the summer of 1985 the 09.58 Manchester Piccadilly to Brighton and the return 18.48 Brighton to Derby services turned up with Class 45/1s. One week in June it was almost a solid set of Peaks. Here we find No. 45131 waiting to depart Brighton with 1M41, the 18.48 to Derby. After finishing my shift in the travel centre, I could get home, grab some food, get back to the station, catch this train to Gatwick have a pint at the airport and then catch the 14.00 Leeds to Brighton back home. Lovely! Taken on 18 June 1985. (A. Gibbs)

Montpelier sidings has a strange collection of bedfellows today. Railfreight grey No. 47367, Thameslink unit 319030 and preserved 4SUB 4732. Taken on 10 June 1988.

No. 33001 has charge of an unidentified return excursion from Brighton to the London Midland region. In the nearly empty car park is what is thought to be a London Country RLH bus. This is probably there due to the London to Brighton historic commercial vehicle run on this day. Taken on 5 May 1985.

Brighton saw plenty of excursion traffic and here we find No. 47136 recently arrived on an unidentified Merrymaker train from the west. Taken in 1977.

EPBs were not common visitors to Brighton except when the London to Brighton bike ride was on. They were used to transport riders and their bikes back north. They were later used on a regular parcels and mail working and here we see 4EPB unit 5421 at Brighton on just such a service. Taken on 20 August 1986. (R. Marsh)

In the Parcels dock at Brighton we find Nos 09015 and 73117 along with another unidentified Class 09.

A very clean No. 09017 trundles into the platform at Brighton with an ex-works Mk I TSO coach and brake van. Taken on 6 July 1974. (J. Field)

Sporting a pair of non-standard white painted discs, No. 47157 accelerates away from Brighton with 1M64, the 15.20 to Manchester Piccadilly. Nice bit of clag too! Taken on 27 August 1981. (A. Gibbs)

Trailing a sister unit SR 2HAP No. 5604 departs Brighton on an East Coastway service. There's a nice selection of 1960s and 1970s cars over the fence in the car park. Taken in December 1972.

Berthed in a long-gone siding next to platform 10, also removed, is 2H DEMU No. 1120. In the gloom of the station a 2BIL can just be glimpsed. Taken in January 1969.

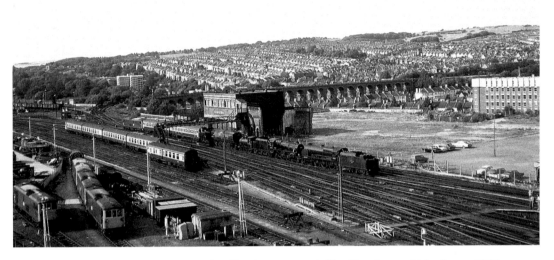

A cavalcade of stock can be seen outside of Brighton station. A Class 73 and two vehicles from a 4VEP are used to propel several steam locomotives from the national collection into the station. 10 July 1976.

Brighton station and Lovers Walk Depot staged regular open days through the 1970s. In the station we find No. 09023 and the brake down crane tool van, which was used as a barrier vehicle to get the exhibits out of the former Pullman car shed at Preston Park. More photos of this later in the book. Taken in July 1976.

Most of the locos stored at Preston Park either ended up in the National Railway Museum or on heritage railways. Locos seen here include King Arthur No. 30850, Black 5 No. 45000, Beattie Well Tank No. 30587 and No. 34051 *Winston Churchill*. Taken on 3 September 1977. (A. Edwards)

Another exhibit stored at Preston Park was this Waterloo & City line battery locomotive DS75. Behind it is LSWR-liveried M7 number 245. Taken on 3 September 1977. (A. Edwards)

The motor coaches from Brighton Belle set 3053 were also brought in as an exhibit. They are sandwiching the catering car S12529S from 4BUF unit 3084. This was claimed for the National Collection and stored at Preston Park for a while. It later moved to the Nene Valley Railway for some restoration work in 1978 but sadly was damaged by fire there in 1978 and the remains were eventually scrapped, a sad loss to preservation. Taken on 3 September 1977.

Beattie Well Tank No. 30587 is one of the exhibits in Brighton station. Built in 1874 this locomotive is part of the National Collection but can normally be found at the Bodmin & Wenford Railway in Cornwall. Taken on 3 September 1977. (A. Edwards)

Arriving at Brighton on a Merrymaker excursion from Cleethorpes is No. 47428. It doesn't look like they've brought any decent weather with them. Taken in May 1979. (A. Gibbs)

Trailing out of Brighton is 2HAP unit 6062 with two unidentified mainline units and possibly another 2HAP. There was a regular afternoon working to London formed of 2HAP, 4VEG, 4VEP and 2HAP, which this could be. Taken in August 1981. (M. Howarth)

No. 33022 is highlighted by the winter sun as it passes Brighton signal box working 1M64, the 15.07 Brighton to Manchester Piccadilly. Winter 1979. (A. Gibbs)

In bright sunshine No. 09003 takes the empty coach stock off the 'Manchester' into Top Yard. The photo is taken from the station switchboard. Unusually, there is no stock berthed in front of the window to block the view. Taken in April 1984. (A. Gibbs)

Fire! British Rail had a huge private telephone network and still does. One short coming was that 999 calls could not be made direct and had to go via the local switchboard. It was my turn this day to take the call from the traffic regulator that Brighton signal box was on fire. After redirecting the call to the emergency operator, I grabbed my camera for a couple of photos. A former colleague of mine, John Atkinson, also took a call in 'the control' from the box saying they were getting out! We still don't know who took the last call. The fire caused serious damage to the signalling, but a limited service was up and running very quickly. Taken on 1 October 1984. (A. Gibbs)

Network Southeast was formed in 1986. Over the years they had a number of special days where you could travel anywhere for a pound. Needless to say this caused huge amounts of overcrowding on the first one. Later Network Days had extra trains laid on and were more expensive! No 50023 *Howe* powers out of Brighton with a return additional train to Oxford, I think! (A. Gibbs)

Inside Lovers Walk Depot. On the right is 4VEG No. 7902 without its Rapid City Link logos. In the centre is an unidentified 2HAP and to the right a 4CIG. (A. Gibbs)

No. 09023 and the Brighton breakdown crane tool van are passing the carriage washer at Lovers Walk en route to the former Pullman car works at Preston Park. Taken in July 1976.

No. 09023 and the tool van from the Brighton breakdown crane are used to reach into the former Pullman car works at Preston Park. The first catch is Beattie Well Tank No. 30587. There are lots of engineers' wagons in Top Yard. Taken in July 1976.

You couldn't really get a busier scene if you tried. No. 09023 leads a cavalcade of preserved locomotives away from the Pullman car works. A 4VEP hurries northwards. An unidentified Class 73 has a long train of flat wagons loaded with concrete sleepers and rail. There is a train moving through the carriage washer and another berthed alongside the Pullman car works. Taken in July 1976.

Classes M7, Q1, the Waterloo & City loco, King Arthur and a Black 5 are all being prepared to shunt back and pick up another loco outside the Pullman car works. Taken in July 1976.

The Beattie Well Tank and Battle of Britain class loco are now added to the ensemble, along with Electro-Diesel No. 73122. Taken in July 1976.

Behind *Winston Churchill* and bringing up the rear is No. 73122. Taken in July 1976.

In the lower goods yard at Brighton we find 2BIL No. 2090. This unit was often brought out for various exhibitions. Looks like wagonload freight and the Royal Navy today! In the background the former Pickfords store had become the Brighton branch of Comet Electrical. This landmark building has sadly been demolished. I purchased my first bit of hi-fi from there ... well I say hi-fi, it was an Amstrad twin deck cassette player with big piano key controls. Taken in May 1978.

Looking back at Lovers Walk Depot from the bridge in Dyke Road Drive. 2BIL No. 2090 is trundling towards Preston Park. Plenty of parcels vans in Top Yard. Taken on 10 September 1977.

Looking south again from Dyke Road Drive an unidentified Class 47 powers away from Brighton with 1M50, the 09.20 to Manchester Piccadilly. A few CCTs and GUVs plus the local Class 09 can be seen on the left-hand side of the mainline in Top Yard, along with VEG, VEP, CIG and HAP units in the depot. Top Yard signal box cabin was later removed to the Bluebell Railway and re-erected at Kingscote. Taken in autumn 1980. (A. Gibbs)

Catching the low winter sunshine on a frosty morning at Preston Park, No. 47487 heads 1M50, the 09.20 Brighton to Manchester Piccadilly service. Taken in winter 1980. (A. Gibbs)

An interesting view sees LNER K4 steam locomotive No. 3442 (61994) passing Preston Park signal box. The locomotive was power for 'The Marquess Goes South' railtour. One of the Brighton Belle sets can be seen in the distance. Taken on 12 March 1967.

Preston Park station buildings were demolished around 1971/2 and replaced with a wooden 'CLASP' structure. The 'new' buildings consisted of north and south waiting rooms, plus the ticket office on the Up platform and a waiting room on the Down platform. Only the ticket office and a bit of the down waiting room structure remain.

2BIL No. 2090 is being used on a shuttle service, presumably between Brighton station and Lovers Walk Depot on an open day. Taken on 10 September 1977.

No. 09005 waits to depart Preston Park with the 'Three to the Sea' railtour organised by the Class 20 locomotive society. The railtour had originated at Sheffield and Nos 20064, 20030 and 20118 are on the other end of the train.

A few photos from my favourite photo location in Brighton. Mill Road, Patcham. None of these images are possible now as the A23/A27 interchange and forty years of vegetation block the view.

An unusual but booked formation for an afternoon Brighton to Victoria semi-fast service. 2HAP, 4VEG, 4CIG and another 2HAP still in Patcham Tunnel. My first car, a Vauxhall Viva HC, can be seen in the car park facing me. Taken in December 1980. (A. Gibbs)

Powering northwards No. 47534 leads 1M64, the 15.20 Brighton to Manchester Piccadilly. It was quite common for a Mk II TSO coach to be in the formation. Taken in 1981. (A. Gibbs)

Now formed largely of Mk II stock No. 47143 exits Patcham Tunnel with 1M64, the 15.00 Brighton to Manchester Piccadilly. Taken in 1983. (A. Gibbs)

Looking northwards at Mill Road and the rolling hills of the South Downs. A very unusual visitor to Brighton is 'Tractor' No. 37109 working an excursion train from Great Yarmouth. Taken on 5 December 1981. (A. Gibbs)

The afternoon sun catches a 4CIG, 4BIG formation working a headcode 14 Victoria to Brighton semi-fast service. (A. Gibbs)

Heading south for a Brighton station open day is LT electric locomotive No. 12 *Sarah Siddons* towing preserved 4SUB 4732. Taken on 15 July 1983. (A. Gibbs)

No. 33061 and a very clean rake of Mk I coaches head south at Mill Road with an excursion from the Midlands. Taken in 1982. (A. Gibbs)

Heading north is an unidentified 4VEP working a stopping service from Brighton to Victoria. Taken on 22 May 1980. (A. Gibbs)

Heading towards Brighton is a 4CIG, 4BIG formation forming a semi-fast service from Victoria. Taken 1982. (A. Gibbs)

Having spotted the alteration in the weekly traffic notice, a quick drive out to Mill Road in the Vauxhall Viva got me this shot of an unidentified Class 33 working the Salfords to Fawley empty fuel tanks. The train was diverted along the coast due to engineering works. Taken on 9 August 1980. (A. Gibbs)

The 08.15 Littlehampton to Victoria exits Patcham Tunnel and crosses Mill Road. The train is formed 4CIG, 4BIG, 4CIG often shortened to ICBC in the carriage working books. Taken on 9 August 1980. (A. Gibbs)

Taken from further up the hill at Mill Road than my usual position, No. 47534 coasts towards Brighton with 1O74, the 07.27 from Manchester Piccadilly. Taken on 3 September 1981. (A. Gibbs)

The famous north portal of Clayton Tunnel and 4VEP No. 7734 enters the 1-mile and 499 yard (2066 m) long tunnel. Traffic along the A273 makes taking photos here just a bit risky. Taken in August 1976.

A bright sunny day at Hassocks and 4CIG No. 7318 departs northwards. Hassocks station was a concrete 'CLASP' type structure, which was replaced a few years ago. Taken in September 1983.

Crompton No. 33015 makes a fine sight as it clatters through Hassocks with 1M13, the 18.25 Brighton to Manchester Piccadilly service. Taken on 6 May 1988.

Taken from the foot crossing between Hassocks and Burgess Hill stations. 4CIG unit 7307 heads for the coast with a Victoria to Brighton 'fast' service. Taken in May 1981.

Nightingale Lane, Burgess Hill, and we find No. 47147 working 1O74, the 07.27 Manchester Piccadilly to Brighton service. Taken on 31 August 1981. (A. Gibbs)

Once again at Nightingale Lane, Burgess Hill. 2HAP No. 6028 leads three other 2HAP units south on a London Bridge to Brighton working. Taken on 31 August 1981. (A. Gibbs)

4CIG No. 7320 leads a twelve-car formation on a Victoria to Brighton fast service. The location is Nightingale Lane, Burgess Hill. Taken on 31 September 1981. (A. Gibbs)

Keymer Junction, Burgess Hill, is where the line through Plumpton to Lewes branches off the Brighton mainline. Here we see an unidentified Class 47 lay down some clag after a signal check as it heads south with the Ardingly to Westbury stone empties. A London-bound twelve-car EMU passes. (D. Burton)

Curving on to the Brighton mainline at Keymer Junction No. 47826 heads north with 1S76, the 08.55 SO Eastbourne to Glasgow Central. Taken on 23 June 1990.

Departing from Wivelsfield station 4CIG No. 7345 heads towards Brighton with a semi-fast service from Victoria. Taken in September 1985.

A deserted Wivelsfield station sees a London Bridge to Brighton service approaching formed of 4VEP unit 7871. Taken on 14 March 1981.

Snow on the ground at Haywards Heath as 4BIG No. 7042 waits to depart with a southbound service. Taken in March 1986. (A. Gibbs)

We go back in time a bit to 1963. Adams Radial Tank No. 488 and E4 473 are captured outside of Haywards Heath goods shed. They were working 'The Spring Belle' railtour, which ran from Victoria to Sheffield Park on the Bluebell Railway via Haywards Heath and Horsted Keynes. Taken on 31 March 1963.

Rail replacement bus services are nothing new. Outside of Haywards Heath station we find Southdown Queen Mary 953CUF and an unidentified Bristol VR waiting for passengers. The Southdown bus station can just be seen behind the buses along with a Volvo 240.

No. 73004 *The Bluebell Railway* has an unusual job today. A gauging train consisting of a pair of 'Queen Mary' brake vans sandwiching a MK III sleeping car covered in polystyrene blocks. I think this was in conjunction with the introduction of the Thameslink Class 319 units on the Brighton line. Taken in 1988. (A. Gibbs)

On 13 June 1988 No. 56062 was working the Ardingly to Westbury stone empties when it passed a signal at danger protecting the branch line at Copyhold Junction, Haywards Heath. The locomotive was derailed at catch points and rolled down the embankment. The leading wagon was also derailed. This view, taken the following day from Old Wickham Lane, shows the start of recovering the train. Taken on 14 June 1988. (A. Gibbs)

Myself and Tim Baker, who I worked with in Haywards Heath Travel Centre, walked down to derailed locomotive via the fields. Here we find No. 56062 on its side at the bottom of the embankment. Recovery was very difficult, and the embankment required some steel sheet piling to strengthen it prior to the crane lifting the loco. The site of this can still be seen today. Taken on 14 June 1988. (A. Gibbs)

With the Ardingly branch curving off to the right, a CIG/BIG formation approaches Keymer Junction with a Victoria to Brighton semi-fast working. Through the summer foliage Ardingly College can be glimpsed on the hillside. Taken on 22 August 1980. (A. Gibbs)

Crossing the spectacular Ouse Valley Viaduct an unidentified Class 47 works 1M50, the 10.20 from Brighton to Manchester Piccadilly. Taken in September 1986.

Maidenbower foot crossing between Balcombe Junction and Three Bridges no longer exists, being replaced by a footbridge. Here we find a grubby No. 47534 powering north with 1M64, the 15.00 Brighton to Manchester Piccadilly. Taken in 1981. No. 47534 was a very common locomotive on these cross-country services. (B. Johnson)

With plenty of snow on the ground No. 33052 has a short engineers' train in tow at Three Bridges. Taken in December 1981.

Class 73 No. E6022 (later 73116) passes the sidings at Gatwick with a long van train formed almost entirely of Mk I CCTs. This is believed to be the van train from Chichester returning to Bricklayers Arms. The headcode should be 9K rather than K9! Taken in July 1974.

An earlier view of Gatwick Airport station with 2BIL unit 2069 bringing up the rear of a London-bound service. This is a hybrid unit formed of a 2BIL Motorcoach and a much newer 'tin HAL' type driving trailer. Taken in the late 1960s.

Another early Gatwick Airport station image as 2HAL unit 2666 pauses with a Victoria to Bognor Regis service. Taken in the late 1960s.

The launch day for the dedicated Gatwick Express service in 1985 was very wet indeed. At Gatwick we find No. 73123 named *Gatwick Express* complete with headboard waiting to depart with the first official service. Taken on 10 May 1984. (A. Gibbs)

1M41, the 18.48 Brighton to Derby, pauses at Gatwick Airport with No. 45126 as power today. Time for a beer in the airport before heading home on 1O86, the 14.00 Leeds to Brighton service. Taken on 26 June 1985. (A. Gibbs)

Jaffa Cake anyone? I liked this livery more than the Network Southeast red, white and blue that was to follow. 4CIG No. 1706, looking very smart, leads a Victoria to Bognor Regis service. Taken on 27 May 1986.

Class 73s have probably had more livery variations than any other class, pro-rata. Here we have Nos 73111 and 73114 both sporting corporate rail blue as they wait to depart Gatwick for Victoria. The number discs were to show the trains diagram. Seven sets being required for a full service. Taken on 7 September 1984. (M. Kerry)

1986 saw an increase in the Brighton line Cross Country services to four trains in each direction, including a daily working between Newhaven Marine and Manchester Piccadilly. At Gatwick we find a near ex-works No. 47459 working 1M00, the 12.15 from Brighton to Liverpool Lime Street. Arrival time at Liverpool was 16.27, just 4 hours 15 minutes from Brighton. Looks like there's a curtain flapping out of the window. Taken in summer 1986.

No. 73142 *Broadlands* in 'executive' livery has just arrived from Victoria and an unidentified Class 73 in 'large logo' livery waits to depart with another Gatwick Express service. Taken in summer 1985.

No. 47612 *Titan* powers away from Gatwick Airport with a motley selection of coaches forming 1M50, the 09.52 from Brighton to Manchester Piccadilly. Taken in May 1987.

Another view of No. 73142 *Broadlands* sporting yet another livery variant at Gatwick Airport. Across on platform 6 is one of the then new kids on the block a Class 319 on a Thameslink working from Bedford. Taken in October 1988.

We return south to Brighton to head along the East Coastway route towards Lewes, Seaford, Eastbourne and Hastings.

BR type 2HAP No. 6063 waits to depart from London Road station in Brighton with an Ore to Brighton service. The allotments to the left were allowed to go to seed and have now been built on. Taken in 1974. (A. Gibbs)

Kemp Town station in Brighton. Closed to passengers in 1932, and completely to all traffic in 1971, it was at the end of a short branch line. Class 73 No. E6006 (later 73006) has worked into the station with a Loco Club of Great Britain railtour. No. E6017 (later 73111) is on the other end of the train. Taken on 10 December 1966.

The last day the Kemp Town branch was open was commemorated by an hourly shuttle service formed of 'Tadpole' 3R DEMU No. 1205. At Kemp Town we find the unit just emptied of passengers. Taken on 26 June 1971.

With the Brighton Belle sets about to be withdrawn several special trains were run. At Kingston between Lewes and Brighton we find 5BEL unit 3051 working the Southern Electric Group-organised 'Southern Belle', heading towards Brighton on the final leg of the day. Taken on 30 April 1972. (P. J. Fitton)

Arriving at the county town of East Sussex we find 4VEP unit 7730 on a Brighton to Ore working. The station is still sporting its original platform numbering.

4CIG No. 7370 leads a Victoria to Hastings service at Lewes station. Home to the very fine Harvey's Brewery and a Norman castle, which can be seen on the hillside above the train. Taken on 14 March 1981.

Just east of Lewes at Southerham Junction was a cement works. There was a daily trip working to Brighton and here we find No. 73003 working 7C52 formed of Presflo cement wagons at Lewes. Taken in 1977.

No. 33056 *The Burma Star* trundles through Lewes light engine towards Wivelsfield. Quite a bit of snow covers the tracks, although the station staff have made a good job of clearing the platform edges. Taken on 17 January 1985. (M. Hull)

Other than a member of staff Lewes station looks completely deserted on this day. It looks like a 3H DEMU berthed in the Wall sidings. Spot the Southdown Leyland National. Taken in February 1984.

Lewes station and the Uckfield line platform still has track and is being used. 4COR unit 3139 is working an Ore to Brighton service. Taken in August 1971.

Approaching Lewes is 4CIG unit 7330 on an Ore to Brighton service. Lewes signal box closed at the end of November 2019 with operations transferred to Three Bridges ROC (Rail Operating Centre). Taken in October 1984.

3H unit 1107 has acquired Hastings 6L DMBS No. S60022 (from unit 1015). The wider coach of the 3H can be seen as the train curves through Lewes ECS (Empty Coaching stock) to St Leonards West Marina Depot. Taken on 13 August 1985. (R. Marsh)

3H unit 1113 brings up the rear of a nine-car formation working 1M65, the 09.42 Victoria to Eastbourne. The stock then ran ECS to St Leonards West Marina Depot for maintenance. Taken on 10 April 1982. (S. Creer)

No. 73111 makes light work of a single Yugoslavian Railways ferry wagon at Cooksbridge. This is believed to be loaded with furniture en route to the Remploy factory at Newhaven.

With Lewes in the background No. 33106 skirts the River Ouse at Southerham Junction. The loco is working a Wolverhampton to Eastbourne Chartex. Taken in 1981. (A. Gibbs)

Southease & Rodmell station and 2HAP unit 6034 and an unidentified sister unit approach with a service from Brighton to Seaford.

There's not many towns that have three stations on the same line within a mile of each other. The first of the Newhaven stations plays host to 4CIG No. 7388 en route to Brighton.

Looking north from a deserted Newhaven Harbour station. On the left are Sealink ferries *Caledonian Princess* and *Maid of Kent* both laid up out of service. Taken in January 1982.

Looking south from the footbridge at Newhaven Harbour you can see the Marine station. This was used for the boat trains to and from Victoria and the short-lived InterCity service to Manchester. A great array of 1970s and 1980s (mainly British) cars can also be seen. Taken in January 1982.

Newhaven Marine station and 5BEL unit 3053 is on the RCTS Brighton Belle commemorative railtour. The old station buildings are being knocked down and being replaced with a new terminal building for the Sealink ferry service to Dieppe. From the number of Simca cars over the fence, it looks like there is some import traffic through the docks. Taken on 8 April 1972.

The 'new' Marine station and 4CIG No. 7430 waits to depart for Victoria with a boat train service. The view is quite a contrast to the previous image.

Class 73 No. E6048 (later 73141) is at the end of the line, Seaford. The locomotive is in Rail blue livery but with small yellow warning panels. The train is the Bulleid commemorative railtour. Taken on 8 June 1968.

'On the stops' at Seaford is 4CIG No. 7305 berthed for the weekend and 5BEL unit 3053 working the RCTS Brighton Belle commemorative railtour, seen earlier in the book at Newhaven. Taken on 8 April 1972.

Brighton Model Railway Club ran one railtour, 'The Sussex Rambler'. This covered most of the coastal branches including Beeding and Lavant. The train was formed of 73136 and 4TC set 415 and is seen here at Seaford. There's a nice Ford Capri on the loading dock. Taken on 31 March 1979. (K. R. Carter)

It's a fine sunny day in Berwick (Sussex) and 2HAP unit 6042, and an unidentified twin, approach with an Eastbourne to Brighton working. Taken on 3 May 1982.

The 2HAP units had been the mainstay of the Sussex coast local services for many years. In 1982, towards the end of their tenure, they were paired up and reformed into four-car units classified 4CAP (Coastway HAP). At Eastbourne we find unit 3308 (formerly units 6048 and 6066) waiting to depart on a local service to Brighton. Taken in August 1982.

Looking north from Eastbourne station, on the left in the sidings is a Class 73 with a loco-hauled set. On the right is an unidentified 4CIG. Taken in October 1983.

Recently arrived from Liverpool Lime Street is this SAGA Holidays special powered by No. 33035. 'Big windowed' 4VEP No. 7755 is in the adjacent platform. The Golden Rail sign is for the British Rail package holiday company which was based in York. Taken in May 1979. (S. Creer)

Nicely posed at Eastbourne with the luggage barrow is Class 73 No. 73001, the first of a very versatile fleet. Taken in 1985.

Exiting Hastings tunnel is 4CIG unit 7315 with a Brighton to Ore service. The smoky tunnel mouth suggests that a DEMU has recently passed through it. Taken on 22 April 1978.

Departing Hastings, probably for West Marina Depot, is 3D DEMU 1307. Taken in August 1978. (A. Edwards)

At Hastings is the 'Hastings Diesel Swansong' railtour and units 202001 and out of sight 203001. Having just arrived from Charing Cross they will now run to West Marina Depot and back before heading off to Weymouth. Taken on 8 August 1987.

In the bay platform at Hastings is 'East Sussex' unit 207004 (formally 1304). It will be working a service to Ashford via Rye. A nice Mk IV or V Cortina estate is on the loading dock. Taken in June 1989.

6L DEMU No. 1031 is seen at Hastings waiting to depart for Charing Cross. This unit lost its buffet car back in 1964 and was reclassified from 6B to 6L. Taken in August 1978. (A. Edwards)

A cloudless day at Ore and 4VEP No. 7792 arrives there to form a service to Brighton. The track leading off on the left went to the carriage shed which has long been demolished. Taken in December 1972.

Approaching Rye from Hastings is 4L No. 203001. It is sporting a green livery complete with BR and NSE logos. Taken in June 1989.

St Leonards West and 6S unit 1004 arrives on a service from Charing Cross to Hastings. Insulator pots for the forthcoming electrification of the route can be seen strewn around the tracks. Taken on 5 February 1986.

Stormy clouds overhead at Crowhurst as 6L Hastings DEMU No. 1014 brings up the rear of the 09.43 Hastings to Charing Cross service. Taken on 15 August 1985.

Our last view of the Hastings line and 6B unit 1036 arrives at Robertsbridge en route to London. Taken in October 1983.

We now move to the other Sussex Diesel enclave, the Uckfield line.

'Slim Jim' Crompton No. 33206 is found running around an Oxted eight set at Uckfield. It has just arrived on the 1719 from London Bridge. Taken on 30 July 1975.

3D DEMU No. 1315 waits to depart Uckfield station on a service for Oxted and London. Taken on 17 July 1985.

Bright sunlight reflects off 3D unit 1318 as it departs Uckfield. Long queues of traffic built up in the high street when the crossing gates were closed. Taken in June 1972.

Looking back towards Uckfield station an unidentified 3D DEMU waits for the crossing gates to open. The station was later moved to the north side of the crossing. Taken in May 1988.

No. 33046 storms away from Uckfield with an unusually grubby eight set of coaches en route to London Bridge.

A very frosty morning at Buxted and No. 33056 *The Burma Star* calls with an Uckfield to London Bridge working.

Not the usual kind of train to see at Crowborough. Here we find 4TC set 422 with Crompton No. D6529 (33112) on the rear. The combination is working the 'South Eastern Rambler' railtour, which visited Kemp Town and Hailsham during its journey around the south-east. Taken on 22 October 1967.

No. 33037 arrives at Eridge with a London Bridge to Uckfield working. A DEMU can be seen in platform 1.

Out in the countryside at Birchden Junction and 3D unit 1302 curves off the line from Tunbridge Wells West and heads towards Eridge.

We now move across the county to Horsham and set off down the Mid Sussex line and back along the coast to Brighton.

Arriving at Horsham station is 4VEP unit 3877 on a service from Victoria.

In the sidings at Horsham is 4SUB No. 4277 and a sister unit. The train is showing headcode 15 for a Waterloo via Dorking service.

4CIG No. 7394 leads a Victoria to Portsmouth and Bognor Regis service into Horsham.

On the line to Dorking at a wet Warnham we find No. 455839 working a service from Horsham to Victoria via Carshalton. Several sets of crossing closed signs can be glimpsed through the signal box windows.

Trundling south at Amberley is No. 73133 *The Bluebell Railway* propelling the General Managers saloon, a former Hastings unit Buffet car. No. 73133 was the second locomotive to carry 'The Bluebell Railway' name. The nameplates were moved from No. 73004, seen earlier in the book. Taken on 30 July 1993.

Approaching Amberley station 4VEG No. 7908 leads a Portsmouth to Victoria service, which should be headcode 8 not 18.

Taken from the top of North Stoke tunnel near Amberley, 4CIG No. 7369 heads south with a service from Victoria to Bognor Regis via Littlehampton.

At the south end of North Stoke tunnel 4CIG No. 7328 makes a fine site as it heads towards Arundel Junction thence Bognor Regis via Littlehampton.

Passing the shed at Littlehampton is 4VEG unit 7906. The unit should probably be displaying headcode 66 for a Brighton to Bognor service, or 36 for a Victoria to Bognor service rather than 56, which is for London Bridge to Brighton via Streatham. Taken on 7 March 1982.

Stored in the sidings at Barnham is withdrawn 4COR unit 3142. Built in 1938 this unit has been preserved by the Southern Electric Group. March 1973.

A train bound for Bognor Regis departs from Barnham station. The unusual signal box was removed in 2009 and is, despite an arson attack, being restored as part of the clubrooms for the Bognor Regis Model Railway Club.

Bognor Regis at its finest in the pouring rain. 4BEP unit 7006 will form a service to London, attaching at Barnham to another unit coming from Portsmouth Harbour. Taken in March 1973.

It's still wet in Bognor for BR preserved 4SUB No. 4732. The unit is on the 'Seaside Sub' railtour. 4VEP No. 7801 sits in platform 2. Taken on 26 February 1983.

Between Lavant (on the former Midhurst branch) and Drayton to the east of Chichester ran a long standing but unusual freight service. The service used French-built side discharge hoppers to move sand to Drayton to be washed. Here we find No. 73141 heading to Lavant with the empty hoppers. Taken on 18 August 1980.

Approaching Chichester is No. 73141 again with the loaded train from Lavant heading to Drayton. There were approximately half a dozen round trips each day. Taken on 18 August 1980.

Departing from Chichester we find 4VEP No. 7733 working the 12.34 Brighton to Portsmouth Harbour stopping service. Taken on 19 February 1987. (P. Barber)

An ex-works 4CIG No. 7373 departs Fishbourne with a Portsmouth to Brighton service. The round device by the signal box is a mirror so that the signalman can see traffic approaching the crossing.

Passing traffic at Angmering. On the right a 4BIG unit heads a Littlehampton to Victoria service, while 4CIG No. 7397 is forming a Brighton to Littlehampton service. Taken in November 1985. (M. Davies)

The tide is out at Shoreham by Sea as a 12CIG formation crosses the River Adur slowing for the Shoreham station stop. Trains crossing the steel bridge sounded like thunder. (A. Gibbs)

Framed by beached boats a 4VEP crosses the Adur river bridge at Shoreham by Sea with a service bound for Brighton. Lancing college chapel can be seen under the bridge. (A. Gibbs)

With the twin chimneys of Shoreham B power station in the background No. 33003 heads west with 1V34, the 1620SuO Brighton to Bristol Temple Meads. These loco-hauled services were very popular. Nowadays a two- or three-car DMU is used. Taken on 23 May 1982. (P. Barber)

A nice view of Hove B signal box and the Dubarrys factory complex. Hove yard is still busy with coal traffic. Taken on 9 December 1973. (C. Parker)

The signal gantry loaded with semaphore and colour light signals makes a fine sight at Hove as 4VEP unit 7728 arrives with a Brighton to Portsmouth Harbour service. Taken in September 1983.

Frosty sleepers and bright winter sunshine illuminate 2HAP No. 5606 and a sister unit as they depart Hove for Brighton. Taken on 9 December 1973. (C. Parker)

The final image of the book and we have 'Hoover' No. 50027 *Lion* at Hove. The loco has recently arrived on 1O98, the 0550SO Exeter St Davids to Hove, where it has run around its train. Another loco will be attached to the rear and the stock run ECS to Brighton where it will form the 1V12, the 1112SO Brighton to Paignton. I hope you've enjoyed your trip around Sussex.